QUICKSILVER DREAMS

BONNIE BOSTROM

QUICKSILVER
DREAMS

BONNIE BOSTROM

For my beloved Jim,
the days of our life together
pass like quicksilver dreams
melting in sun.

CONTENTS

MEANING MAKERS

There are poems
that cannot bear the weight of words
as the sky cannot hold rain or stop the sun.
These poems are hidden in the heart.
They are dark-eyed glances,
eyes searching for connection
with some longed-for other.
They are direct stares demanding recognition
and a thousand silent words whispered in time.
A dream can carry a wordless poem
all the way from childhood
to unfold in your mind like a play
or a puzzle,
where the clues are constantly changing,
rearranging your past.
Some poems are a gesture; the lightest of touch,
the body speaking the language of "Yes, I am here."
Every poem is a reaching out,
finding a path,
grasping at meaning.
This poem is a wrestling match with words.
The task?
To fashion a clearing here between us
where, together,
we are more than one and less than two.

PLAYING MARBLES
for Bobby Martin

Imagine.
A density no larger than
a marble.
An incredible density;
a marble-sized density filled
with all there is.
Imagine every when, where and what,
all the stars,
color, trees, birds,
songs of birds, river,
rain;
one marble-sized density.

Our sun, its sun,
constellations of suns,
space.
Merely a density
you might hold between a finger
and your opposable thumb.
Now capture this thought in
a net of constellations.
We are within the density,
caught in time, form, and matter.

We reckon by sense
the curving shell of our marble home,
as embryo knows

the containing wall of Mother's womb.
It is the out-boundary
of our being;
and all that is
moves here within a density
no larger than a marble.

Our science tells a reductionist story
of all there is,
and stays,
tethered to a marble ball
for which there is no scale for size.
This science cannot imagine the consciousness
before the density.
Cannot imagine a radiant,
a still point without referent,
a brilliance;
burning,
gathering, moving into being,
becoming the density.

Come inside my mind.
I want to show you a vision that happened there.

THERE IS NO WATER ON THE SUN

The light that touches my skin was born
inside the sun
before earth was born in space.
Moving through the dense belly of that fire,
today's red light lived
in a place that could embrace one million earths.

The light moved,
made its burning way
through new-born space,
where there was no water.

And the center of the earth,
the heart of all we really know,
is pulsing red, and there is no water there.

When we arc wide like a welder's tool
and fly inward to the sun,
the oceans dry
rivers,
lakes,
and all our tears gone to dust,
will there be somewhere, anywhere,
the scent of rain.

BETWEEN WORLDS

The clouds curl like fat cats in the deepening sky
while shadows flirting across the sea's face
leave dark wet kisses in the surf.
There, where the sand and sea meet,
an egret skirts along the foam
searching for succulent bits of food.
We are quite alone here,
this white bird and I.
Together we let the water wash our feet
and share a kinship of hunger.
We feed on beauty
as a flight of brown pelicans dip,
dive,
down from the sky
in unison.
Wing tips touch a wave's curl and they rise,
arcing up, then, catching a drift of wind,
float like dark ships in an invisible sea.
The egret and I, finished with our feeding,
turn away from the water.
It looks at me with ancient eyes and
spreads white wings to sail away.
My eyes join my heart to its flight
and we rise,
flying together out to sea.

CROWS

Surprise held his eyes open
as his wife became a crow.
Her eyes, a usual shade of blue,
grew dark as ants and
slender legs changed to
slighter limbs and spindly feet.
Black gloss feathered from her arms
as her breast shone, down-soft
and sleek.
Reaching across their coffee
she touched him with a tip of wing
and called his name in ancient rune.
From dark within him rose
his own strange singing as he hopped,
bird-footed,
behind her to the nest.

THE SPIDER

The spider, silking her descent to floor
twists her legs to reach at passing space.
Back down, belly skyward the legs turn,
thin twigs in wind,
and the thinner strand holding her life, swings.
Our common solitude breaks the barrier of species
as she pulls me on to ride her fell trapeze.
Back down, belly skyward our legs turn,
spinning inward while the cord drops longer.
It shines silver, glistening
in ageless geometry.
The spider mind is quiet to sleep with
and the dreams Arachne weaves are sweet.

FINAL FLIGHT

Look.
Above the rubble, an owl,
rising pale and gray;
the Bird of Minerva arcing wide to the west.
A shadow
falls from feathers fledged in night
and skirts the edge of light and fire
where men and metal scan the sky.
In its wake
a dimmer moon makes its worn way around the world
and children dream in Plato's cave.
The old ones
see light break like blood on pale gray wings
and watch her fly full circle before the long, long dark.
Look.
Above the rubble, rising fair,
the Bird of Minerva arcs wide to the west.
A fell hue falls on her and ancient light
from stars extinct, crumbles into color on her wings
as she glides ever more westward.
Once before, this bird took flight
and Rome remembers
as we now see,
the Bird of Minerva flies at dusk.
The owl lay on the dark highway,
death a final pinion for wings

once loosed in flight.
Picking it up, she remembers the deaths of her
mother, father, other loves, and a far distant time.
Tears fall like the soft dirt she covers over it
as she breathes out, "I release your spirit."
The myth runs deep that wisdom is embodied in a bird.
It follows us down through time
and deep, the cutting away of symbol from the source,
for it was Minerva who was wise
and the owl belonged to her.
The old goddess bends down to toss the last
of dust upon gray wings, and watches as her bird,
flies higher and more far, than ever before.
Look. Above the rubble, rising fair.

INITIATION

I see them standing in a circle,
the dark suits.
They look pressed and crisp
as though the silks and linens
of their lives are sorted out
and shining straight.
They walk in a field of
stubble grass,
stern dark stains against
rare small shoots of green.
They are darker even than their shadows.
It is the meeting of a mystic order
and their black ritual jerks the day
into closer focus,
rimes the day with light shining like ice.
The sound of their celebration sifts through
cactus flowers and sage,
making its own space as it moves around me
and catches me
in a web of language I think I know,
and yet I find
it is impossible
to understand
the conversation of crows.

FISH OF SILVER

Skinwalker casts his turquoise shadow upon this land
and ghost dancer, sliding across the rocks like rain,
dances us up from blood turned silver in sand.
Spider Woman weaves a lasting web for us;
the stars are points of patterns that she drew
when first her lips reached down to kiss the dust.
Fisher man, dragging her nets across the sky
traps planets and persons in this gentle snare
and decorates his mother's designing
with his light.

WAR

Roll the sound of sacred aum inside your mouth
and breathe it
backward. The word
falls into the world as rain might fall from a red sky.
This world holds the sound of war inside its mouth
and speaks a secret mantra
into the dreams of children as they sleep.
Some may hear the scythe of time
severing light with dark,
splitting life into points along a spectrum of pain,
like when the bombs fall into your arms,
or your feet are freezing off
while you walk the winter road
through hell.
There is holiness in the world;
the inhalation of the divine breath
as it pulls you into the dark is holy. Life is sacred,
but death is holy.
A million miles away from Earth,
do prisons look that different
from the extermination camps in Germany
during that war?
Gas chambers, electric chairs, injections.
We exterminate, kill or take their
lives away from them
one day at a time as they do time; a silent

and unholy war.
Bring the view into sharp focus,
lie down next to the man waiting to die,
hold his head in your hands
feel the wild pulse at his forehead;
wrap yourself around him
like a chain. Grant him his dying wish;
he does not want to go alone.
There is a war on the horizon,
sounding like the heartbeats
of a thousand horses,
like a tank in your doorway,
like a mantra
made backwards.

ANOTHER WAR

The heroes are gone,
the fields have drunk enough of blood
to slake the thirsting Earth.
The sun casts no shadow where once
the shape of trees drew birds like dark
compasses pointing to shade.
What once were rivers of blue and clean,
with the dear dark green of growing things
upon their banks,
are roads that yield smooth rocks worn old by water.

Even if the rains should come again,
mix with the red stain left by lives carelessly flung
into hot eternity,
flowers will not bloom here,
and Earth will not give herself to seeds.

Nothing will dredge life from these bright plains.
Sun will change the dirt to clay,
peel the flesh away
and birds, mistaking the dark and silent forms
for shade,
will peck away for marrow in the bones.

There is a low ridge in the distance,
merely a rise, a soft upward slope
that yields the track the heroes made
when they left a world behind.

THE DISTANCE TO DISTOMO

It could be measured in miles or the years
that have passed
since, in a frenzy of vengeance,
the Nazis killed all two thousand villagers
of Distomo.
Here in this beautiful valley,
a mute monument to the dead of Distomo rises.
A marble message tells a story of such sadness
that my heart stiffens and cannot beat.
I read the names, ages of the dead;
there was no mercy for the young.
Infants, women, all; there was no mercy,
no one left to grieve them.
Tears fall into my hands and I hold them
until they fill, flow over the sides and fall,
turning to light before they touch the ground.
They are a river flowing into Distomo;
a river of rainbow light
moving on ground that trembles to receive mercy.
I turn away to see blue sky shining like grace
over the village of Distomo;
in my hands I carry rainbow shards,
the residue of merciful grief.

BANG! THE BOMBS BURSTING IN AIR

The sky blooms in light
brought through time
from the land of Genghis Khan here to Boulder,
where we celebrate the 4th of July.
We took bright victory from our father England,
Boom, left their dead to be buried
without flowers or family.
Try to remember the light
as it struck the soft grey suits
of the dead and wounded
in the sad lost South, oh Dixie, Bang!
Or the blaze at Normandy
where the sea ran red, bright
as any firework flower.

See the light on forgotten faces of babies in Vietnam.
Are those roses or blood,
bright on the white shirts of their fathers?

Look, a television rerun of the glorious
lights of war, in the night of the same
sky that spreads from Berlin to Boulder.

Boom, a child falls –
flowers bloom in his mother's hair,
his sister is a dance of flame,
his uncle carries a daughter, dead,
and his father lifts a gun to fire.

Oh, oh look.
There.
A beauty; a flower blooming
in the sky. It glitters,
it glows and falls
fading toward the earth.
A child races toward the horizon
to catch a falling star.
Their faces shake in the light.
Oh, Earth
falling apart, the seams dividing
in bright red blood and
the light of fires burning
away their brotherhood.

Oh bright, oh beauty.
Bang, Bang, Bang the flowers are falling,
the falling,
the bright, the bright, the lights,
the fall of tears,
falling, bright as blood.

SOMETHING GREEN FROM 1969

I didn't tell you much about the Berkeley days,
or Monee,
and how she let me brush her hair
with my hands, comb it
and slip a beaded barrette
into its black depths.

We were in Oakland,
wounded;
she at Alcatraz, I in the streets.
We were easy friends, linking our lives
for safety, sharing food, water, words.

She was a Cree woman
grieving for the northern timber
country in Canada
where all the green trees were being bought
to make matches.

I imagined the red-tipped sticks
bursting into tiny flames,
imagined the great green branches of pine
leaning far too quickly toward the earth,
groaning and splitting,
falling like silent soldiers to the ground,
their long trunks smacking the earth,
snapping off at the base,
the green boughs,

the green needles falling wordlessly,
mute,
and green.

She blessed me and gave me a name I did not
understand
until years and miles away
I ate the powdered green bitter buttons of peyote,
drank the willow bark tea,
and watched as it rose,
from within the circle of us all.

The peyote bird is green.
You see them with turquoise inlay on silver
but the one I saw rising is more than bird,
more gold than green,
more light than form;
there is no name.

I did not tell you about Monee,
a Cree Woman,
and how she let me touch her hair
before she flew away.

PEDERNAL
for Barbara Martin

Take my body to the low plain
that lies beneath the Pedernal.
The schist atop that great mesa forms
a citadel of stone,
a stranded city of rock
shading the Northern slope down to Abiquiui Dam.
Obsidian and the deep green of Ponderosa
form dark color on the Pedernal;
in noon sun or the cold moon of winter
the mountain is always black.

Below the foot-rocks, in the dark home of Earth
Mother is making a gift for me.
She plunders the ruby veins of her body,
the sapphire tears that crust her eyelids,
diamond teeth,
garnet lips;
her own emerald eyes will be perfect.

She makes the stones,
extracts the gold from meteors that pierced
her tender skin.
Lapis, turquoise, topaz,
opal and amethyst,
she strings on long strands of her onyx hair.

Mother is beading a necklace for me;
the design an intricacy of jewels
from her body.

Take my body to the low plain
that lies beneath the Pedernal,
lower me down into mother's arms
and I will begin
to make a necklace for my daughter.

RED BIRD AT RED LIGHT

The light turns red at Beach street
so I stop,
face off with oncoming cars,
think briefly of Siamese fighting fish
and what to fix for dinner.

In the breathless hold before the arteries fill
and the flows shift
from north and south
forming tributaries, west and east,
a flash of red is juxtaposed
against rows of metal and brittle glass;
a singularity of life,
her movement that of the deeply real.

She has migrated from beachside,
navigated the bridge in wind,
is here,
before the glass where I sit trapped
in quiet metal.

My eyes know the street is filled with noise,
with noxious fumes;
her lungs are small, she is fragile.
Her heart is beating, pumping red blood
against the chemistry of air and exhaust.
Sun strikes her head, glints crystal,

a sheen of light
as her tiny feet land sure-footed on the curb.

The artery is a fast moving river now;
my mind in even faster time
knows these cars and others yet
will run to rivers of rust,
bleed their red lives down
into the crust of the earth,
last, long after she and I are gone.

My eyes turn to find her again and there she is:
Dorothy,
adjusting the neck of her red sweat suit,
pushing back her crystal hair,
checking her watch for running time,
continuing West on Granada Street.
The light turns green.
Time to go.

ABBIE AND ANNE

Abbie Hoffman talks to me in dreams
and when those images surface from
night's easy fold into straight bright thought,
I know he did not kill himself.

They found him fully dressed, in bed,
with his shoes on.
Was this modesty imposed upon his final act,
to save his friends from grisly intimacy,
from seeing his virility made vulnerable
in the extreme emasculation of death;
his sex and life cut down at once?

Vanity.
Perhaps he understood his flesh would hang,
crumple into natural poses;
wanted to shape his final form to fit convention;
avoid Adam and Eve nakedness before God.
He accepted guilt with clothing.

Or maybe somebody murdered him.
He says America did it, hammered his heart apart
like copper sheeting, beating against his brain
with frame after frame,
the picture always the same of hate,
and justice decided by tipping the scale
towards greed.
He shows me how his heart

exploded in grief,
a fragile puzzle, the seams unzipping,
contents moving apart slowly.
The divisions are like ocean water
between Africa and South America;
his heart was larger than all the seas.

He takes me to Anne, touches her hair,
and wanders back to his bed, fully clothed.
We cannot live in Anne Frank's little room.
There's not enough space for all of us and
the flowers there are dead.
They die the instant they are cut off; murdered.
Flowers are the sexual parts of plants.

In my dream, Anne and I gather flowers
from a million graves; the petals are dry and sweet.
We know those whose bones lie in these graves
did not commit suicide;
they were murdered, we say, they were murdered.
Now we gather flowers, this dream girl and I,
placing them in gentle bundles on our backs.
We carry them a long, long way to water.
We scatter them on the water separating Africa
from South America;
we scatter them on all the oceans,
on all the oceans and all the seas.

FOR GARY ANDERSON

The dreams start,
made of fire and urgent images of people
free,
and places where rain is not spattered
with the blood of children,
where their parents do not read
dark shadows in the sky
as portents of danger.
Those are not planes, merely large birds
winging home
in sun shattered sky.

They change,
the dreams become almost visible banners
we bear like armbands for grief
or a remnant of some thought
Joan of Arc may have fought for
and delivered into her fire.

The dreams live apart from fathers
crying for their babies
and mothers searching the empty fields for wheat
or small jewels of rice.

They catch us if we are not careful;
lodge in our hearts like claws,
the dreams.
They enter early on and even while we spend

our tears and savage artistry on talk,
we cannot help but feel the fire
curling and burning the sky.

And the dreams?
The dreams
drench us with destiny,
drive us in the search
to find rice,
eat the pain,
trade art for bread,
turn blood to wine
and clear the sky
of birds of stealth and prey.

THE SILVER SHIP

The moon hammered on my window with a silver fist
broke through and cut across my room like a scythe.
Is this death riding on a silver ship
that has come to greet me so?
No, it's the dream I had when I heard
the Earth crying in her sleep.
What tears are these
falling on my blue midnight sheets;
whose grief is roaming around my room
on a silver boat?
Is it Charon come to row me across a river of light?
Whose death has awakened the dread boatman,
whose cries called him in the night?
This grieving is for the dream I had
of rivers and rain when they were sweet
and birds breathing easy in the air,
a dream that came in green and danced like water
in my room, that came in a red sunset
and the deep blue of a cobalt sky so clean
I saw the ocean reflected in it.
The boatman catches the last green branch
of my dream,
casts a long net to pull bright tears from the bed;
silver fish from a cobalt pond at sunset.
I heard the world weep.
I heard the Earth crying in her sleep.

LIGHT RIDER

I wonder if you waited all night for dawn to arrive,
knowing you would begin a journey then.
The night could not have held your flight
and so I picture you, all your work done
here on this plane,
readying yourself for departure.
You spent precious hours,
sifting through your history for any chance shadow
that might have contributed to the cancer.
Each small dark thing you pulled from your heart
and let go into light.
We are always departing,
running from dark things that awaken us in the night
or stop us, breathless,
in the bright sun of ordinary day.
We run from death
but it is always death we are running toward.
Yes, I picture you
poised like the marathon runner you were,
right at the horizon of dawn, at the edge of light,
and I can see you running, running free,
out of the reach of darkness.
You lift easily off the earth,
catch the sun at its rising.
This is what you were born for, Cassandra.
You were born to ride the sun.

MEETING AGAIN

I saw her face reflected.
The wide shining windows at The Top of The Mark
sent it to me against the backdrop
of San Francisco lights.
I knew she was remembering
her dervish days, twirling and spinning
round a windmill pipe.
She had seen Saturn make his seven-year trek
full three times and
was celebrating having negotiated the turning.

Once she was wearing a hat
that stopped my heart
when I spied her
in a storefront glass as I strolled along Grant Avenue.
It was improbably filled with flowers
on a brim so wide it caught ocean mist and twilight
and I'm sure I caught the scent of sea foam
as she *paso dobled* past.

Mexico was good to her.
I saw her brown-skinned and freckled
boarding a late flight from Oaxaca to the States.
Her smile said a thousand secrets had been spoken
in the hot sand
and the hot air
on Playa Del Ropa.

She loved jazz in the City.
Everyone from San Francisco calls it the City
and she loved the City.
She has smiled that love to me
from the bottom of a glass of Scotch "neat"
while she listened to Cannonball Adderley
and told outrageous tales
to attractive strangers
and old friends.

She danced.
The Contemporary Dancers Workshop
on Polk Street
was a harbor for her heart
and anchored her gypsy feet to the Liebestod
from Tristan and Isolde.
Everyone applauded for days including me.
I'm not sure she heard.

I lost touch with her, as we do,
and then,
just the other day, while driving,
I heard a cut by Cannonball Adderley,
and there she was
with me
where she has always been.

FOR BROTHER DAVID STEINDL-RAST

She takes the napkin
folding it
over
and over,
careful of the
crumbs of cake that cling
to it
like grains of yellow sand
or
tiny bits of saffron rice.
The scent of destiny
fills the afternoon,
mixes with the tea
and honey talk around the table
where Helen Siegl dispenses gifts;
a wood block print for every guest.
The napkin is bundled,
bound tightly and slipped
like secret silver into the dark
of her pocket.
It is for love
this thievery of
trash and scraps
is done,
and there is no witness to accuse her.
All afternoons

become the sweet of evening,
turn to final night,
but this day is ever etched in light;
the day she stole from a Saint.
Perhaps they play out past lives
they never lived,
maybe the future never happened.
All she knows about any of this
is that when Brother David dies
she will open the napkin
mix her tears with cake crumbs
and share her feast with him.

JOAN HALIFAX ROSHI

This woman
is not simple.
Even her laughter
holds the crystal
complexity of silence.
Her eyes
draw water from the well
of my heart.

THE NETWORK
*"Do not refer to Me as the Creator. I am the Creating,
and everything is Me, changing My mind."*

INSIDE THE MIND
The constellation cells,
planets, suns and thoughts
inside the mind creating,
creates me.
My mind inside the cell can see,

THE EARTH
This cell, with its
outer shell of bathing light
and water, clouds and sky
trees and sea,
calls to me.

THE SOLUTION
Expressed in chemistry,
written in light,
the clouds and amniotic atmosphere
swaddle the Earth.
Earth, living cell of such sentience
that it speaks a tree;
an entire vocabulary
of leaves and green.
Such vocabularies and language
has the Earth
that it will speak me.

INSIDE THE SOLUTION
The solution is expressed
as fire, air, earth and water,
moving. And moving,
man and tree
rise above the surface
where ocean touches sand
and mountains lift from water's grip
to stand before the moon.

THE NETWORK INSIDE ME
Each time; arriving.
A light, a click of fire,
ticks and flames,
connects the patterns,
blankets the brain in layers,
links fire to star to cell to seeing.
The chain of network thought
inside the mind, creating,
creates me.

EGG-CELL SELF
The galaxy swirls in space
and dots and pricks of light
pin-point my way.

The egg encloses each wandering light
and turning round and bout this center self
is shut inside
then rolled down the flight pattern
of mother's borrowed belly
into the womb
and broken open by sperm-cell me.

SPERM-CELL SELF
Daily,
taking flight and arriving 200,000 strong,
the children.
As the clouds, sky and light watch my
sperm-cell me flying into the constellation,
thousands will be with me,
flying toward the egg.

PLANET AS EGG
Swimming toward the egg,
a million and more,
we surround the silken circle
and the corona of sun swifts and
swirls and spots break, burst and bloom.
The planet egg is bombarded with 200,000
conceptions and the sperm are home.
Stars are born this way.

SELF AS SEA-HORSE
Sperm-cell me
spent in fusion union,
burrows toward the egg.
Deep within mother's belly
the coronation,
and swirling whirling merry-go-round
with golden sea-horse me,
I ride the cloudy sea to Earth.

MET AT NETWORK
Inside a new mind, a cell;
itself neither come from
nor going into anything,
senses,
finds me there.
The multiplication of me
thus met in conception
fire-fused in union,
sees rising,
the warm globe of mother's face
her eyes are green and trees,
moons I see
set in a constellation face.

ARRIVAL
Outside now,
I see my reflection in this
face of Earth,
reflecting,
mirroring back to me
the journey to her arms.
My birth at any stage was only me,
shedding the amniotic shell,
embarking in space-cell capsule me,
penetrating egg-shell Earth,
jettisoning the tail
of rocket ship sperm and traveling
always, always in the cosmic
fluid movement of
space-time,
only me,
traveling home.

ALIEN

I am not at home on Earth.
The night sky should look familiar,
the sun would not burn eyes
born of this system.
The praying mantis, moose and crocodile
could be close friends
if I shared with them Earth's design.
I resign myself to displacement
and longing
as I view unreadable trees
and am confounded by the road
from seed to flower.
In exile I wait,
hoping in some way to make passage home.

A STORY THAT DID NOT HAPPEN

I'm using invisible words for this.
Real words might cause pain,
sound like rocks thrown into water,
or seem like lies.

I had an apocryphal childhood.
No one remembers the facts,
and if they do, they change them
to fit some authentic dream.
Each sibling saw from a different life,
the jagged jigsaw puzzle we
carved out of time.

The shadow of my father
lurked in corners and under the bed
where it joined my dreams.
Sometimes it fleshed out for summer visits.
He was young then, too.

I was scrawny-ugly, wore
my lack of beauty like a banner.
It offended my mother
whose beauty was armor.
I made the usual Mandalas of wild flowers,
laying them so every
petal faced the sun.
Then I would lie,
East to West inside the magic center.

Hunger was a childhood playmate.
At night, lying beside me
I felt her chill fingers
caressing my belly;
my bones were cold with want.

Once there was food left
from a simple supper and my eyes
followed the bowl as
it was tucked like treasure
into the wooden cupboard.

That cache of shredded cabbage
lay that night between me and hunger,
the dream of its pungent perfume
following me to bed,
the room thick with scent of vinegar and onion.

I took the hand of my old companion and
eased into the dark, quiet
in the sleeping house where all my siblings lay,
my parents, the dog.
The dog paid no notice
as my feet carried my intent
to the kitchen and as
my friend and I reached toward
the bowl, the words slapped
against my pounding heart like rocks.

"Get out of there," the voice startled
the dog, mute witness to our shame,
our shaking humility, when we stood
to steal food from our family.

I was homeless once
or near, making a home
deep inside a condemned hotel
in Pueblo, Colorado.
Forty-four empty rooms; my daughter
skated in them and down long hallways,
her blond hair bright and dangerous,
should someone see it shining
through the windows.

We came and went at night,
our shadows blending with
ancient shade of trees by moon.
The bathtub served for laundry,
dishes, bathing.
Bless the man whose crime of engineering
made electricity our single luxury for the hot-plate;
but not for night,
when light could alert the law.

There was no way to clean;
the dust was older than my life
and more intractable.

It was summer and when heat drove us out,
we waited until there were no cars
on the street, no people.
We liked the old railway station
where the cool had a thickness
like water.

We discovered wild spinach in the yard.
It meant food.
We ate it boiled with pieces of salt-pork until
the city mowed down the weeds; we hid inside
for two days, afraid they might return.

My son ran away from his father's home,
hopped a train and tried to make it to me,
preferring poverty and love
to anything else he knew.
He made it from San Francisco to Reno.
He came the whole way, for good,
at twelve.

I cannot throw old cloth away;
remnants have their stories.
and I remember-

Mother curling our hair around simple strips
made from old clothes
and tying them so people at church

would know she tried to manage
our straight, rebel hair.
Mother, on her moon,
folding soft muslin to protect herself.
Mother cutting old clothes,
tacking pieces together with yarn,
our familiar shirts and levis
worn again at night
as quilts for winter cold.

Mother with a J crochet hook,
making rags into rugs,
holding her babies in the cast-off clothes
of older children
and making underwear from softened flour sacks.

Now at night I sleep
in old t-shirts my husband lets me steal,
and there are doilies in my home;
tattered lace given by a sister,
her gift a precious story.
I cannot throw old cloth away.

These are not real words
and the story is not true;
no story ever was.

HARD DOG

Ranger was a hard dog to love.
He seemed to want freedom
immediately after the door closed,
or affection when I was dressed for work.
I frequently felt he used our friendship,
leaned hard on my tendency
to be intimidated.
He did all the things I dislike in
a dog.
He barked at cars,
insisted on sitting on the couch,
demanded food when we were eating,
and fought with other dogs.
After his last fight
he lay in the shade of the house
dying in a quiet
foreign to his history.
His eyes met mine and showed
a knowing I've seen in human death;
he was leaving, going someplace else
and could not rise to goodbye.
My eyes dropped first
and letting go,
I loved him.

MASKS

I have worn many disguises.
Once I was a seven year old girl
afraid of nothing,
who could fight,
bite,
lie,
and beat up anyone in my class.
At ten
I could run 3 miles barefoot on a dirt road
and not give out,
but got my feelings hurt when I wasn't chosen
for a team.
I've masqueraded as a bride,
a mother,
and worked as a police clerk matron.
Once I had a dancing school,
lived by nobody's rule but my own,
and was surprised at being a grandmother.
I've been a majorette and tossed my baton
as high as the best of them,
played at getting drunk at high school picnics,
and run away from home.
I've taught school,
x-rayed people with bullets in their bellies,
and held the hands of people as they died.
All these masks and more

I've worn,
all the while
rubbing against myself
like an old bear against a tree,
trying to find out
what's inside the disguise.

UFFIZI GALLERY

I stand humbled by art.
My heart crumbles into small breaths of devotion
as I stumble through this gallery.
My eyes have created a living triangle
between my brain and heart,
where a river of images run wild.
I had ever longed to see Bacchus
as Carravagio
had seen him, and now that visage
is transformed from a small picture
captured in a book
into shadow, form, light and color,
recaptured by my eye and given to memory.
As a child
I wanted to make images,
create beautiful shapes, but my desire
could not translate paint or crayon or clay
into beauty.
I comforted my craving with words,
hammered my heart out in black on white,
trying to show the same
deep red human heart
I see in every piece of art.

RED RACER

The snake twists,
a red electric dance beside the road,
and in stunning time
the snake and I run
down arroyos
we both have known.
I am nine, barefoot and hot,
walking on mud cracks
among the sunflowers.
There is a cool spot where
water has lingered a little
and left a slickness of mud.
Digging my feet into the wet
I smell a sweetness of earth
and water mixed and am held by the scent,
not really seeing,
when a blaze of crimson moves
before me and stops.
My heart echoes in that halted time
a thousand times.
We see each other, the snake and I;
our gazes meld and run
even further back, to the garden
where we first met.

MIGRATION

We stand beneath
the flame maples of fall.
Arkansas is gold and fire,
lying at our feet in Mother's yard.
Our shadows splatter;
ink on leaf,
as we plan for birds.
I lift the blocks and place
their gray faces
one on one.
The feeder will be high
for viewing from her window.
We stop,
caught by the patterned flight
of great migratory birds,
soundless, bound for home.
I bend to lift again
and turn,
she should not see
my tears drop upon the block.

In her house I check for latent danger, worrying
over the sinister shift of throw rugs,
slippery tile,
and rumpled carpet.
Walking the short way to her mailbox
she teases, chides me to write.

I walk in other times when the child I was
witnessed the beauty of her dreams.
Some dreams are finished;
her books printed up
and locked in time upon her shelves.
New dreams, poems, she reads aloud to me,
a weave of music, symphony of sense.
She is my muse.
Flying home,
seeing the last green glimpse
of the south from a small window,
I sense the force and form
of the steps we take
toward final migration.

I WANT TO SLEEP IN WIND

I want to sleep in wind.
Not the wind of Southern summer
wrapped sweet and soft
by the wet lick of lilac and mint.
New England breeze sifted through leaves
blooded by the touch of winter,
is insufficient for these dreams.
Northwestern wind;
ocean, pine drenched and damp,
folded with flocks of gulls and geese
is not my yearning.

Give me Southwest wind.
The wind that burned and scoured my childhood;
the hot summer scald of air
moving through cactus spine, sunflower stalks,
and barrow ditch thistle.
Wind filled with the sound of brown snakes,
twisting wind,
grinding through milk weed;
the silk becoming liquid stars
or long thin snow.

I know that wind so thick with dust
and the little stones that ants collect,
so thick that noon stars are caught in its fist
and held before the sun.

I have felt the sting of sand against my skin,
brought by the sudden gusting of a whirlwind.

Sometimes the shape of wind
is a long blue sheet of rain
drawn against the unmoving silence of sky.
The smell of water washed by shattered sage
drifting in slow wind;
I have wanted that smell so deeply
that I have sucked stones
picked up in city lots,
my nostrils primed for a rush of rain.
I have prayed for rain.

In winter, the wind whipped sounds the livestock
made against the windows where I slept.
The cold frosted my dreams with those sounds;
cows, the dog barking back at a coyote's thin call.
Wind drifting, singing, piling snow into mounds
into rounds,
like a dancer's clothes; wind is always naked.

So take me when I am dead to any Mesa,
wrap me in sage and thistle down,
fill my mouth with small stones,
my hands with rain.

I want to sleep in wind.

HIGH PRIESTESS

It is evening.
Light and dark are swinging in the balance
and as the scales tip toward darkness,
millions of stars spill into sky.
Centuries ago men addressed the firmament;
with line and angle, myth and animistic art
they affixed upon the stars their alchemistic auguries.
Tonight my mind will not fit into those designs made
before the pyramids,
before Plato, before me.

I have the right to read the stars,
to reject ancient connect the dot patterns
that seem a limit to my soul.
In the West I see my mother's rocking chair
and to the North my father's saddle.
I connect the lines between the stars,
find familiar points are the angled designs
of Navajo rugs we laid upon as kids
to watch firelight flicker from the coal stove
lighting the ceiling cave above our heads.

The southern stars are a story my mother told
of when the moon fell in love with the sun
and the stars grew small with jealousy.
I am an astrologer who has walked the stars,
seen evening become the warm gold spill

of morning,
and made my own magical mythology.
It gives me joy, keen and sweet,
to see my mother's kerosene lamp
rising in the East,
my father's black horse loping into the West.

GALLERY HOPPING

After the fifteenth painting
my eyes long for the comfort of
space filled with stars light years apart,
want white walls, and
empty window sills or an ocean in the North.
This art is raw and inedible
like the fish in my mind.
A school of fish, twisting and
darting, is moving in fluid color toward
the street outside; outside, the street
is filled with cars all flowing to points away,
reminiscent of the big bang.

Some people look at paintings,
strike poses,
check to see who's seeing.
The punch bowl is brilliant
with tangerine drink and pieces
of lime are floating belly-up like
dead fish in a sunset pond.

Mints, all colors, are motionless
in their rounded bowls.
They look like fish eggs or a still-life by
someone who has eaten lobster and
wiped greasy fingers on pastel
napkins.

I grab a tangerine drink, three mints,
and some peanuts,
as I swim past the sixteenth painting.
Knowing you're behind me
I dive beneath the noise then rise,
break surface,
and head for the stars.

VISION BASKET

I decided to weave a vision basket today.
I want to capture you inside it when you say your
words into the air.
I will travel in my mind
to the arroyos by the White River
on the Apache reservation.
I'll gather red willows
like I did with the Jicarilla women
who taught me their basket secrets.
I have a sharp knife to peel bark
for twisting tightly
so I can hold what I catch of you.
I know you put your heart in your words.
I see you bend over paper with pen or pencil
putting your heart and mind together.
That's what I'm doing.
I'm twisting the willow peel of my mind and heart
together for this special basket.
Poets are always giving their hearts away,
peeling back layers of their lives.
So I make this basket like a net.
Your words will be fish in ocean air,
swimming round and round until they fall
into my basket.
I will keep them safe,
like I always do

when I catch a little bit of you.
Usually I tuck all your words away inside
secret files and drawers I keep open,
but tonight they are going home with me
in this red willow basket.
You deserve something special.

CARNIVAL

I had strung carnival lights
on all spaces where you would see me,
arranged their sequenced rhythms to blink or glitter
to suit my hair,
fed you cotton candy,
put new paint on the merry-go round ponies.
I polished the golden ring;
you said you liked the circus.

At times the distance from the high wire is so far,
you look like a shadow on the ground.
There have been dangerous breaks,
falls of subtle magnitude,
moments when you have seen me in sun.
Unprotected by special lighting, real light
betrays me to you.
You see the lines on my face filled with time's shade,
hear my voice more like my mother's than my own,
and my costumes need enlarging, serious repair.

It's the trapeze work that scares me.
Fear of falling grips my fingers and
each night brings dreams of the circus closing.
I want to know,
when my hands slip from time's fastening
and I fly miles above the crowd,
how will your hands find me?

DUET

I knew the moment Mozart entered my dream.
The backscape changed
from burgundy to brilliant blue
and his smile shook my heart as we melded,
morphed, moved together as one.
Soundless music entered next,
falling around us like crystal rain,
like a hurricane's tongue,
like velvet ribbons and satin streamers
from a volcano's mind.
I recall waiting for the sound
that did not come
and did not come
and Mozart moved our feet toward a piano
that was always there but never seen.
We had no audience, but millions waited
just outside the dream
just outside of time.
The backscape changed again
from blue to living flame
and when we touched the keys
with burning hands,
I understood what it is to organize fire.

THE WAY OF TITANS

I take trees,
make lattice-work lace from twigs fallen to ground,
festoon my feet with the greenest leaves
and bracelet my wrists with soft bark sheaves and
Spanish moss.
Clay from river beds; crimson, deep and red,
becomes bright lines upon my cheeks and brow.
Captured stars nestle in the deep recess of every curl
and my hair is a blanket of light.
I'm waiting in the almost dark
when day bleeds out the last of sunlight.
You are coming to me
with a necklace of shell, feather, stone
and the whitened bones of small creatures.
You will plait my hair, taking care that stars
do not sear your skin.
Then, remove the bracelets,
wash my face with rain,
let the crimson clay drip upon my breasts.
Your mouth will know the way,
say my name in secret language
as your hands find my fire.
I will hold you fast,
enfold you in light's soft space
and cover you in radiance
until the sun breaks us.

FIFTY MILES OF SILENCE

Poverty is hard to talk about
when you are eight years old
and know your family is down to the bone poor.
Circumstance and lack of rain in cattle country
brought my parents to their knees at church
where every prayer began with
"Lord, you know we need rain."
The snows of deep winter
drifted around my childhood dreams
of Heidi and hot bread and goat's cheese
with Peter and Grandfather in the Alps.
There was never enough.
That's the dark face of poverty…
never enough and no one to tell your secret to.
That year when I was eight, it rained,
the grass made good, the cattle sold.
There was enough to buy small,
precious gifts for family Christmas.
While we made our last stop to buy food,
our meager treasures so dearly bought,
were stolen from the bed of the pickup truck.
Our sadness was so deep that on the long trip home
we did not speak.
Fifty miles on a dirt road in a 1937 Chevy pickup;
I could not think of Christmas,
all I could think of was Spring
and the hope for rain.

SPRING IS A TIME

Spring is a time for lavender things,
the hot dark velvet of iris petals in sun,
lilacs dripping over adobe walls in Santa Fe,
and one early bloom
before the Buddha shrine at Upaya.
I kneel precariously before its yellow heart
and feel the smell before it hits my nose,
cool against my flesh.
I know it is coming,
that rare perfume of all my summer memories,
condensed in hot purple scent.
The bloom bends my knees so deeply
you would think I was
captured by Buddha's unwavering gaze.
Instead I am crazed
by the relentless press of summer's mauve
leaves unfolding like days gone to rest in winter.
Those first feet of summer,
slipping into the arroyo's silt after rain.
Those feet, running through sunflower fields
and wild yellow buttercups
on the hillsides of childhood.
Those feet burdened with my body's
weight and the ten thousand things,
now lift me up and I leave that indigo iris,
that summer, this spring, this moment;
still kneeling.

SOMEONE IS RAKING LEAVES

Someone is raking leaves;
the metal tines strike Italian stone
beneath dried twists of leaf and twig.
The music is medieval,
resounding now as it might have
on these same stones
when the street was new.
She is a study in tan and black
carrying her history toward me in a smile,
a slight nod of knowing.
It must be her grandson,
this bright thin boy holding her hand
as they approach the doorway where I stand.
Her perfume captures me.
It is flowers, fruit, joyful and sweet,
a touch of Spring
lingering in late Autumn air.
The street becomes a kaleidoscope,
each brick and stone
falling into place behind her step and
I see her as she once was
when all the leaves were green.

IT IS DIFFICULT FOR A BEAR
TO DANCE IN A BIRDCAGE

My fur fits like a rug
on hard polished wood,
not quite attached,
easy to shift around
inside here where I live.

I don't know when I noticed the cage.

It may have been as I stood
before the door,
inside my home,
and balked at entering the dark outside,
alone.
Or when I chose to screen my calls,
unlist my phone,
avoid certain parking lots,
get double locks.

I don't take evening walks
or watch the sun set, unattended.
I hold my keys like a weapon
while walking to my car,
check behind me as I lock myself inside.

I'm a performing bear,
but was once a bird who flew,
free from every fetter, every fear.

Now I talk, work, make wishes on stars
seen through a window
in my bedroom;
I long for freedom.
Like other captive animals
I overeat,
over consume the safety of television
and video, listen too intently
to sounds made at night.

I wonder if my trainers know just when
I lost interest in dancing
and when the cage closed completely.

THE SONGS OF MEN

Men sing their songs to us as though
our bodies were continents.
Breasts cascade across the country of their singing
like mountain passes
filled with prayer banners and fog.
Hair eyes, mouth –
somewhere in there they sense
a woman whose juices are rivers, lakes, laving
water.

Lotus and lily float above the streams
of tide-pushed, moon-pulled blood.
Dirt, pebbles, grit and groin;
the crocus blooms in their hands.
Red-lipped roses pulse,
throw their perfume like verses in a new book.
Thumb, teeth and tongue, a fantasy
and dream clouds are green
like sheaves moving through ground.

They spice our eyes with colors
borrowed from a trout's turn in sun.
Sand is tiny glass, seen as shining skin to lay upon;
the beach moves into the sea.
Hollyhocks and paintbrush find themselves
together with bluebells and berries
blooming in haiku,

fragrant gifts in seventeen sounds.
Dark trees are secrets on a hill, sweet
as sun and warm as arroyos after rain.
Our arms are branches, vines, circles filled
with their shoulders;
an entire civilization born of nesting birds
soars like words through their poetry.
Our hair, bright as light at dawn
or deeper than ebony
is panther, gull's beak, cinnabar or burned gold.

Their songs to us, in strains
of midnight sound, define our ears
while that music scents our hands
like summer limes.
It is a mystical country we become,
larger than any life we really lead,
when in the delight of their discovery,
men sing.

ANOTHER IMPRESSIONIST PAINTING

Their movements have been
choreographed by Seurat,
they've been stolen from the picnic scene
on the island of La Grande Jotte,
are here,
come to life in my midnight window.
Mother, father, child.
This trinity adrift outside my sleepy window
speaks in pain and stilted screams
come out in sentences repeated:
"Bring my son back to me now."
"Bring my son back to me now."

He carries the child slung on his hip
like a Koala Bear on a eucalyptus tree
away, and then back to her.
They go into their dream door,
and it closes for a time while sleep wraps me
again outside of time, until
there is such red inside
my room and flash and
doom sounds of doors
opening and a child's voice
threads through the sounds
of other people and into
my sleep.

My dream is the textured
landscape of Seurat's design.
He kindly holds my hand
as I stand on the Island beside the Seine,
the scene framed by my window.
Then I watch as the artist
adds red and a stretcher
and the jagged dance of
a little boy running in his
underwear between the eucalyptus tree
and his mother who is limping
now as the Seine recedes in the distance.
The sunbathers have taken all
their colorful umbrellas down and the
mother won't get on the stretcher.

Seurat has saved his signature use
of yellow paint
for the last few brush strokes.
The sun rises as the ambulance
disappears into the screaming
light of morning.

THE DAUGHTER OF A HUNTER MUST BE BRAVE WHEN FACING DEATH

for Jiggs Collins

I did not think of your death yesterday
and how you sat upright
in hot August
and thought it had snowed.

You lay,
fettered by machines, their green readings
a dark forecast.
Each breath you fought the dark for,
wrestling the air into your lungs,
lying still to keep the needles from slipping
from your veins.

At times you listen, as for some predator
outside the window.
I see your dream in the room.
You walk through a stand of aspen,
following the track a deer left in new snow.
Your breath is easy on the air,
catches and holds when you see him,
As the big buck falls,
blood runs death red on the snow.
You leave some on traps you set out for coyotes.

The machines go off in the room
like they've trapped something massive

and as the nurses flock toward your bed,
I watch you gather your traps,
turn and go,
out toward the mountains
In deep August snow.

DINING ALONE

He sits two tables away,
a handsome old gent, still wearing his scarf.
He takes the bowl, the glass,
the napkin from the tray and places them just so
and begins to speak in a low voice.
I avert my eyes,
wait for his prayer to be over.
He bursts into song only for a moment,
begins to speak again.
As he eats
the fragments of song break forth and stop, he talks,
chats amiably inside
the small world of his table.
My mind supplies ample reason for him.
He misses her,
and how she used to laugh at his operatic attempts
as he addressed the soup with familiar phrases
and he tells her important news of the day…
she had never learned to read.
She listens, nods from time to time and her smile
is everything he has ever loved.
I watch as he tidies up the table for the two of them,
the bowl and glass back to the tray,
napkin folded into its original creases
and once more he surprises her;
a short phrase from La Traviata, her favorite.

He puts on his great overcoat,
adjusts his scarf and smiles toward the table.
Just as he opens a door to the street
his heart opens fully in song and
I hear her laughter echoing back
into my heart.

THE DANCE

He pulls her up out of the wheelchair,
directs her arms around his neck
as he asks her to dance toward the chair.
She follows his lead and lets her feet
shuffle a *cha cha cha* forward
then stops,
waiting for his cue.
He turns her body slowly,
a simplified swing step that ends with
her safely in the car.
Once back in her room he sits beside her
lifts her hand to his lips,
and looks deep into her eyes.
He is looking for his mother,
that bright and sassy woman
who loved fun and word puns and
beat him regularly at scrabble
He is looking for signs that she knows him,
shares their history in memory.
She follows him down the long hall
as he leaves,
putting one foot after the other,
scooting along beside in her wheelchair.
Their strange *pas de deux* is over.
He bends for one last kiss and
looking into her eyes,
sees that all that is left is love.

JUNKYARD SONGS

She skims along the junkyard edge,
scanning trash
for the shine and gleam of glass.
Swinging along she catches
the songs of wind in bottles bluer
than deep Aegean sea is green.
In one, she finds the song
of a sound some late lover
left in her bed.
Spinning in a bucket,
old dust rattles out the tune
time dances to,
and one small vial,
so thin the sun plays on the song inside,
tells of a secret place
hidden twenty years ago behind a glance.
She takes them home, the bottles,
to line her window sill for winter,
when she will listen to them singing
and pour their sun into her hands.

NOLI ME TANGERE

She could not touch her beloved
or know the scent of his body
lingering upon hers again,
or move, fully alive
within his embrace.
It is always the same,
the sadness of women caught
inside a madman's dream,
daring to believe
the dream is true.
And this dream?
To be immortal,
taste the eternal, know infinity.
Mary Magdalene's tears fell that day
on Earth,
the only heaven she knew was real.

SIGNS ON THE ROADSIDE

Seen at sixty miles per hour, the
hitch-hiker
is a blur, with black shirt
unfurling in the wind like a flag.
Stop?
No, you barely have time to see
his teeth and lips
locked in the please position.
Your foot hovers in confusion
above the brake
and you can't let go
of your breath.
Yield?
The temptation to take the time,
turn,
reverse the gears and ask
the flag inside
pushes your foot with fear.
At seventy the flag begins to fade,
merges
with the rest of America
disappearing in the rear-view mirror.

MICHELANGELO'S STONE

He embraces that silent, square,
immobile stone
with anxious hands.
Searching, with swift and skillful fingers,
he knows the cold contours of its shape,
the clarity of composition.
His sweat and mind
are one upon the rock
mingle in flowing form
beneath his final movement.
He breaks life from stone.

A WORD

I launch this word across the dark heart of silence.
It has escaped a thousand gravities to reach my lips,
the gravities of war and death, of suffering and pain.
I send this word like a ship through space,
cutting its way through the molecules and atoms
between us
like a rocket moving through planets toward the sun.
I cast this word out toward you
across the mystery of time
where we have played out our human trysts
and tragedies,
where we have fought, risen and fought again.
I send this word that I caught with my heart,
as it flowed
through the rivers and tributaries of my body.
This word is invisible, seen by spirit only,
the last to fly from Pandora's box.
The word is hope.
Hope that we can rise again in strength,
to push against the seeming night
that gathers ever near,
hope that we can find each other in time,
join,
find a fulcrum of power within us
and unleash our peace upon the world.

OUTFIELDING

The words dance
sing in my head like ice-shine on lakes
long frozen in winter.
Making their way to my tongue takes
longer than sunlight moves
to reach my morning face.
I watch the rise of light
upon my planet,
and there,
just beyond the reach of sun,
some strange familiar darkness.
The dark hands of God are always there,
playing catch with the sun,
and letting us watch the game.
I've been running bases since the beginning;
there was no bang,
nothing,
no one there to hear the tree forever,
forever falling, forever
in the forest falling.
No one to see
when light was a novel written in clabbered stars
clotting into a language in bas relief,
a Braille book typeset on dark time.
I slide into Saturn's rings (safe again)
wait to make my way.

I intend to steal home.
The moon knows this game; sees me,
with the face he hides from earth,
sees me, rolling
round round round
the outside infield of space
orbiting,   orbiting,   orbiting.
I have always known the sun's embrace.
She has kissed me brown and warm,
left small planets on my face and arms in summer
been my sanity's anchor when the cold was bleak
and the winter long.
So I head out again
again again again
from the same place, never the same space.
Sisyphus is reborn daily before the same mountain
rolling a ball he has never touched.
Everything is always new, always,
new under the Sun.
I am the Sun
and I know that just ahead,
always just ahead,
just there;
here;
almost here almost here almost here
the Catcher's hands.

LOVE, DOORS, AND ROSES

I pull the door almost closed,
gently,
sending night time kisses to my babies.
The door opens and "I love You"
precedes my daughter
as she slips into my arms, easily, at eight years old.
"I love you Mom, he says as he walks to the door.
a man, now in his middle years,
much larger than ever I would
have imagined.
My daughter, now grown, calls
and I hear my granddaughters in unison:
"I love you Nanny."
My mother's voice laden with the scent of roses
echoing after me for years, her last words,
"I love you guys."
My father's door closed hard behind him
while he slept.
"I love you, Dad," followed the silence
that lasts forever.
My grandmothers' voices still call,
outside time's door,
"I love you." "I love you,"
I've saved all the roses.
The pictures they colored and brought home,
running through all my doors.

"Here, I made it for you Mom. See, it says I love you.
Roses. It's my valentine to you."
The roses from my father's grave,
bright crimson words saved in a satin box.
say I love you.
And you, my love,
I will say it to you
before every door that opens in our life
I will say it, say it, say it until every door is closed.

COMPOSTING

I slip the tines of the pitchfork deep into the dark soil,
Shifting, sifting, the dirt and small tufts of grass
Over scraps of food
Saved carefully for this heap.
Worms, uncovered, exposed as they work,
Wriggle like snakes,
Disappear into the wet earth.
There, just before me, rich green leaves,
Long and slender, catch my eye.
Onions.
Green onions have volunteered here on the heap.
Bending down, I marvel at their presence.
Somehow a miracle has happened here.
A garden; a garden of four green onions.
Like a little family.
Something moves me at the core
As I pull them from their dark home,
Taking care to preserve them intact.
The white tube, the hydra roots at the bottom
Still clinging to tiny grains of sand and dirt.
A thousand and more generations of women
Bend with me,
Gather the food into their arms,
their bowls, pots, aprons, and garden baskets.
I feel them stir within me,
These women who nurtured seed and flower, who took

Dry husks of corn, rice, tender lettuces
And the ripe red berries of fall
And brought them inside for winter.
In cave, tent, yurt, and hut, rock house and brick,
The wooden shack, the half dug-out
They brought their garden glories to the table
As I now bring these small and wonderful plants
Into my home.
We sit down for a simple lunch,
These women of other times and I.
Relishing this simple harvest,
Remembering.

JOAN'S DREAM

It was almost April
Five Hundred and Thirty Nine years
after her fire,
In Oakland,
that Joan and her men appeared.
Her horse was weary, the men
tired beyond reason.
Why her horse was white,
and why they all were out of time
did not occur to the mind
of the mad housewife
who knocked on every door
begging help for Joan and her men.
Juxtaposed against the grocery store
on a timeless corner of the world,
she held her banner aloft.
Crimson or scarlet or burgundy it bled
its red color across the entire world and no one came
to aid the housewife
who saw so clearly the need for food, for water;
the horses needed hay.
She ran to them, to join them
but the distance between them stayed the same,
ever the same.
Now the housewife sometimes sees Joan
the Joan not yet a saint,

astride her tired stallion, holding bright
the banner of her life
and once quite recently
she received an invitation
or an image
or a vision
or a sign inside her mind.
A band of metal like a thimble
open at either end with raised rows
run round and round
and *fleur de lys* encircling;
a memory in metal
the housewife could not catch
reach or touch.
But someone told her the story of the arrow
and what it was
where it came from and what it did.
How it was fletched with feathers,
and the feathers held by a metal band;
a metal band on the arrow
that flew through her sky to pierce Joan.
The invisible arrow struck, soft as feather down
the *fleur de lys*
unfolding in Joan's heart
filled her blood with longing
for the invisible world

that housed the bow,
and the archer.
It flew again through time, without an arrow;
an idea, an image almost remembered or forgot
that lodged in the mind of the housewife.
She is going again to every door
begging help for Joan, for her men;
water, please,
the horses need hay.
She is running forward in time to join them,
And the distance between them now
is not so far
is not so far.

THE CARE OF LAMPS

I've never trusted electricity.
I am at ease with the dark,
drifting through my rooms now
as I did in childhood.
We used coal oil lamps then.
The corners of the ranch house
were softened by golden light;
the flame a living sun in every season.

At seven, Mother let me carry the lamp.
Fully aware of the danger of broken glass, oil,
and fire,
my little sisters trailed cautiously behind me
to the bedroom where we
read for awhile before sleep.

At Mother's urging, I would cup my hands
behind the globe
and blow gently into the glass
and there, fire and air mixed for a moment
before the flame died and dreams
slid into bed beside me.

Everything seems closer in darkness.
It's the dark that delivers our imagination,
midwifing visions of light, transparent chimera,
and the diaphanous truths of childhood.
Cleaning the lamps held special dangers

for our hands.
The globes were fragile, had to be held firmly
while wiping the inside with a soft cloth;
no smears, no smudges allowed.
The wick had to be trimmed.
A small gear rotated the wick
so we could cut away the burned cloth;
soot would darken the lamp glass and nearby walls.

Filling the lamp without losing a precious drop
or letting it spill down the sides was a job for two.
My sister held the lamp and funnel while I poured,
stopping at just the right moment
before the oil rose too high.

Then the lighting. The burning match flared
like a brief comet and then the wick caught fire
and we had our own small sun,
shining, warming, seeming to become brighter
as night deepened.

At night we got up without the lamp
so taking in detail is automatic; an unconscious
adaptation of pattern recognition.
I notice small things, indiscernible to eyes
addicted to the blare of incandescence.
I can map the house,

take a mental picture of everything in my home,
so that now, at seventy.
I can rise in the dark,
fix early coffee, and
wander freely. The blind have no choice
but this is my preference.

The fabric of my favorite chair is different
in darkness, its contours greet my body
like the welcoming arms of an old friend.
I settle into the dark, pulling up dreams,
letting my imagination recreate my sisters' faces
illumined by remembered lamplight,
hearing their soft breathing as I
read them to sleep,
and at times,
it seems I hear my Mother's voice
calling from a distant room,
telling me it's almost time
to blow out the lamp.

SEVEN POEMS FOR SAPPHO

THE DOORKEEPERS FEET
ARE SEVEN ARMLENGTHS LONG

I stand on his shoulders; measure the reach of his
arms as he churns the sea to frothy anger.
They are twelve chariots by horses drawn, deep
into water.
The door is there to guard Poseidon's daughter
whom I have seen swimming in the greenest sea
and love has brought me brave to gain admission
into her room.
I know the way through wave and foam
the path is redrich and golden; her hair in radiance.
The map I gleaned from golden birds lost, flown wild
into my nets.
The keeper will not see me dive and glide soft as
down on swan's wing to Poseidon's diamond cave.
At sunset's death I'll cleave the water's mantle
into the deep.
I will free her from a jealous father's keep
below the verdant Earth where every flower
waits and weeps in joy for want of her dear birth
into the world.
I will kiss those ruby tresses that I've seen both
in dream and light, the bright dressing of Dawn's gift
to Aphrodite,
when she walks from the sea onto shore.

APHRODITE'S KISS

The one with violets in her lap
sifts through the dusts of time to find raw
mauve and fragrance trapped
within the silky skin
of violets.
She twists each petal into tender stain and paints
a thin magenta line; a stanza, dark with love
adorns her mouth.
Just now gold sandaled Dawn breaks
like ruby rain and fire; it falls on shoulders
bare and breasts, her hair.
Thus the morning star
brighter by ten thousand times sees,
reaches down to kiss violet lips.
Aphrodite, showering Sappho
with prismatic starshine,
transforms those flowers into light.

STAY

Sweetbitter unmanageable creature who steals in
silent as snow on Olympus,
you disrobe my sight.
I sense, more than see
your midnight hair, the stir of which
is music.
The fleet footed thought
that you might leave before day's first light
pulls my hands to your hair.
Take crimson ribbon and burnished gold,
braid our tresses together tightly
then bind
our bodies with satin sash.
Stay Sappho, sweet muse,
share the remnants of this pale night with me
for we are sweetbitter creatures of word and song
and I am mad for you.

THE COMB

It must have fallen like a star from night's embrace,
a dear treasure slipped, escaping your perfumed hair
as you left.
Intricate jade and amethyst
latticed with soft laces of pink gold and porcelain;
it is evidence you were here.
You walked deft as deer along the narrow hall
carrying garlands of blossoms you used so
fetchingly, to trace the contour of my face,
the soft bowl of my belly.
Your evening fragrance lingers like a song on the comb,
and as I touch the golden teeth to mine,
the sound I hear is love wrought and rife with want.
It is not the body enduring this deepest desire,
nor my heart, nor mind.
Sappho, it is my soul's own self in longing.
It is the fire that breathes me into life;
the wildfire that burns all that is not you
from my reckoning.
I press the comb into my lips, remembering,
until the tiniest jewel of red joins the jade
and amethyst; a kiss.
When night comes next you will know this gift,
and the fire that drew the garnet droplet from my lip
when, soft as sun on thistle down
I'll take the comb and kiss your hair.

GOLD ANKLEBONE CUPS

Some sacrifice is intended for these chalices
fiercely designed from the dear dead bones
of birds that flew
once free and far above all thought of shore.
When captured,
caught in my nets of silver lace,
their songs were sky and flight;
live arrows transfixing the quicksilver moon.
And no more than the bird with piercing voice
cuts through the night in death,
do I cut these nets when the songs are gone.
Binding their whitened bones with saffron hair
you left adrift on morning pillows, I fashion
the tiny cups, ready them for secret rites.
Come, I've drawn my heart's bow,
tethered my love to a sparrow's foot
and filled the anklebone cups
with gold.
When your lips curl round the cup of amber wine
stop;
recall the songs that died for this.

THE 10TH MUSE

She glides through cypress trees in white,
her robe trailing like satin wings folded
after flight.
Slim golden feet that I have kissed,
barely touch soft moss and earth
as her skin embraces mist and green.
She sings to the moon.
Like a Tibetan Lama, she knows her music
will live through time in the moon's light,
and enter the mindstreams of other women.
As she lifts her lyre in song,
archetypal rhymes and melodies
mingle with mist,
form shining mythic pictures;
Carmen, Isolde, the dying Mimi,
and La Traviata are born in the
glistening woods.
When the moon is more ancient than tonight
and Sappho's light and mine are gone
women in a different world will sing
moonsong and moss,
satin,
and the sweet green mist on golden feet.

LOVE REMEMBERED

Papyri taken from the long dead in Egypt
have your words on them, Sappho.
Unwrapping corpses of the long dead
explorers knew what gold they held in trembling hands,
knew the truth of treasure.
Lovers placed your poems on the bodies of their darlings
a magical protection against impervious death
and the long wait for heaven.
They pressed your poetry against flesh that would feel
no sweeter kiss than Sappho's songs along their bones,
no embrace more tender than love remembered in verse.
Each fragment stands as witness
to the Goddess of Lesbos,
whose words were lightning, sea, wind, and cattle,
whose songs echo in the sands of Egypt, and in my heart.
Thank you dear muse with hair of raven's wing,
your beauty is all I need of art and knowing.
As you before Aphrodite stood,
a supplicant, I with bended knees
offer you my songs,
and this poetry; a bouquet of quicksilver dreams.

Published by the CANELO PROJECT
www.caneloproject.com

Other Books by Bonnie Bostrom:

The Way Showers *(with Joan Baliker)*

Women Facing Retirement: A Time for Self
Reflection *(with Barbara Reider, PhD.)*